MW00748985

VOLUME 3

Sports

Created by The Church Art Works

ZondervanPublishingHouse
Grand Rapids, Michigan
A Division of HarperCollinsPublishers

Zondervan / Youth Specialties Books

About the YOUTHSOURCE™ *Publishing Group*

YOUTHSOURCE™ *books, tapes, videos, and other resources pool the expertise of three of the finest youth ministry resource providers in the world:*

• *Campus Life Books—publishers of the award-winning* **Campus Life** *magazine, who for nearly fifty years have helped high schoolers live Christian lives.*

• *Youth Specialties—serving ministers to middle school, junior high, and high school youth for over twenty years through books, magazines, and training events such as the National Youth Workers Convention.*

• *Zondervan Publishing House—one of the oldest, largest, and most respected evangelical Christian publishers in the world.*

Campus Life
465 Gundersen Dr.
Carol Stream, IL 60188
708/260-6200

Youth Specialties
1224 Greenfield Dr.
El Cajon, CA 92021
619/440-2333

Zondervan
1415 Lake Dr. S.E.
Grand Rapids, MI 49506
616/698-6900

ArtSource™ Volume 3: Sports

Copyright © 1991 by Youth Specialties, Inc.

Youth Specialties Books, 1224 Greenfield Drive, El Cajon, California 92021, are published by Zondervan Publishing House, 1415 Lake Drive, S.E., Grand Rapids, Michigan 49506

ISBN 0-310-53841-6

All rights reserved. The artwork and contents of this book may be used and reproduced without permission from the publisher for its intended purpose. It may not be used or reproduced, however, in any other books or publications having a similar purpose, without the prior permission of the publisher. The republication of this book in whole is prohibited, and resyndication of the content in whole or part without written permission — for resale in the form of negatives, positives, mats, printing, etc. — is expressly denied.

Created by David B. Adamson and J. Steven Hunt of The Church Art Works, Salem, Oregon

Printed in the United States of America

91 92 93 94 95 / ML / 10 9 8 7 6 5 4 3 2 1

**Enter a New Era of Creativity
With ArtSource™ Computer Clip Art**

The clip art you see in this book is also available on computer! Youth Specialties and The Church Art Works invite you to try computer clip art—high-resolution art on computer disks for use with the most popular page layout programs. Each illustration is digitized into its own file for easy manipulation—stretching squeezing, enlarging, and reducing.

Enjoy the advantages of creating the electronic way—with ArtSource™ computer clip art.

COLLECT THE ENTIRE ARTSOURCE™ COMPUTER CLIP ART SERIES:
> Volume 1—Fantastic Activities
> Volume 2—Borders, Symbols, Holidays, and Attention Getters
> Volume 3—Sports
> Volume 4—Phrases and Verses
> Volume 5—Amazing Oddities and Appalling Images
> Volume 6—Spiritual Topics

SPECIFICATIONS:
MACINTOSH®: Accessible through page layout programs including PageMaker®, ReadySetGo!™, and Quark XPress™. Minimum recommended memory requirement is 640K and a hard drive. Art comes on DS/DD disks. Also accessible with Aldus Freehand® and Adobe Illustrator® for modifications.
IBM® AND COMPATIBLES: Accessible through page layout programs including PageMaker®, Ventura Publisher®, WordPerfect ®5.0 and 5.1 as well as other programs supporting .TIF. Minimum memory requirement for importing images into your page layout programs is 640K and a hard drive. Art comes on 3 1/2" DS/DD and 5 1/4" DS/DD floppy disks.

ACKNOWLEDGMENTS

Thanks to the hundreds of youth ministers who have submitted ideas for these illustrations. Thanks also to these artists who have contributed to the books:

Bruce Day
Chris England
Corbin Hillam
Mark "Lindy" Lindelius
Dan Pegoda

Also, thanks to our team at The Church Art Works:

Kelley Adamson
Michelle Baggett
Mike Bartlett
Bruce Bottorff
Jeff Sharpton
Beth Weld

And finally, thanks to our wives, Kelley and Kathy, for allowing us to work evenings and weekends to see this dream come to reality.

INTRODUCTION

We've designed ArtSource to be a quick and complete sourcebook for your youth program promotions. It contains art from The Church Art Works' extensive files of ministry clip art, as well as from several other contributing artists. The art is arranged by subject and will cover most activities you'll be involved in during the year. Future volumes will supply new subjects as well as additional art for the current subjects.

We want this book and others in the series to be a real asset to your ministry. You can help us with ideas for more clip art by using the Brainstorm Form on page 14. When you submit your ideas to us, you keep the creativity flowing. We hope our efforts will assist all of you in your ministries as you work for positive growth in your students.

LET'S BE CREATIVE!

This book gives you the chance to be creative, pumping life into your promotions and creating excitement in your group. Just follow these four easy steps:

1. CREATE AN EXCITING IDEA. Planning and scheduling your youth group activities in advance is essential. But don't stop there. Hold separate brainstorm sessions to allow time for creativity to blossom. Creative ideas don't come easily in a "board meeting" format, so get away to a wacky place or neutral territory with a few "crazy" idea people. The clip art contained in this book should inspire some ideas you may not have considered. Once the ideas are on paper, sort them out and plan the logistics later. This will help you break away from the pressures of your everyday work and will keep your ideas fresh.

2. CREATE AN EXCITING MESSAGE. When you prepare your information, think like a kid. Don't be trapped into just listing the "time, date, and place." To expand your thinking, we've shown you some examples of possible ideas on pages 10-13.

BASIC STEPS IN PREPARING PRINTED MATERIALS

Helpful tools that will make your job easier are a pair of scissors, an x-acto (craft) knife, a ruler, a light blue pencil (nonreproducing) for layout, rubber cement, glue stick or wax for adhesive, tape, black felt-tip pens of various widths, a t-square, triangles, sheets of transfer lettering (rub-on type), a technical pen, and a drafting table or drawing board. All of these tools are available from your local art/drafting store.

Photocopy or cut out pieces of art from this book for your project. Choose art that fits your subject. You can reduce it or enlarge it on a photocopier.

Plan your layout. Sketch (on a separate piece of paper) where you want art and where you want copy (headlines and details). See pages 10-13 for ideas.

Use felt-tip pens, a typewriter, or a desktop computer to set your type. Assemble this in combination with the clip art and paste it on a clean white sheet or card for your "master."

Copy the master to reproduce as many printed pieces as you need for your event. Copying can be done on your photocopier or at a print shop.

3. *CREATE AN EXCITING LOOK. Think beyond the "normal" approach in laying out information for an announcement or flyer. Young people love seeing the unusual. Instead of aligning things straight, place them at an angle on the page. If you're comfortable with small type, think BIG type. And if you're tempted to illustrate your message with a normal-looking teenager (whatever that is), use a fat hippo instead!*

As you begin your layout of a flyer or poster, grab a nice big piece of paper, a pencil, and a few pieces of clip art. One way to be sure you don't get trapped into the same old layout procedure is to lay the clip art on your layout sheet first. Let it be as big as you want, just so that it's fun and has impact. Enlarge it if necessary, <u>then</u> work the rest of the copy and headlines around the art. This will create some unusual shapes and column widths. It'll be easier and more fun!

You can also use the paper and pencil to roughly sketch out small (2"-3") layout options. Explore radically different layout of the various elements in your piece. For example, in one sketch the art may be huge with small supporting type; in another, the type may be huge with the art sized fairly small. You have many different options with the same piece of clip art — such as repeating it several times for a border effect.

4. *CREATE AN EXCITING ATTITUDE. After you've committed your plans to God, promoting your event is the first step toward contacting those you want to reach. Stretch yourself and strive for the very best. This new attitude will be reflected in your work. Others will sense your desire for creativity and professionalism, and the enthusiasm will spread. As more people become involved in the project, you'll also stretch them. The results will be exciting, as the "team" begins to focus on a worthwhile goal.*

In the following pages we've put words into action by giving you creative samples of ways to use clip art. Use these ideas to launch your own exciting promotional pieces. Have fun!

IDEA STARTERS

Here are nine ways to use a catchy headline with clip art. Many times the theme may have nothing to do with sports, but the art will get attention and drive home the point. You can add your own ideas to all of the art in this book to continually create new possibilities.

LIGHTEN UP

Be sure to join us for a fun time this Thursday at aerobics. A time to make new friends and have some real fun!

Meet at the church at 9am

YOU MISSED IT!

We had a great get-together last Sunday at our all-city jamboree. We'd love to see you this Sunday for more great fun!
Pastor Bob 555-0000

GREAT JOB!

THANKS FOR YOUR HELP WITH THE PICNIC. YOUR WORK MADE IT ALL POSSIBLE!

HERE'S AN OPPORTUNITY FOR REAL GROWTH

Come to our Wednesday Word Buster where we break open God's Word and share our questions (and answers).

LET'S TALK IT OVER

If you need someone to listen... Call any of our staff. Sue: 555-0000 Bill: 555-0000

LET US BOUNCE THIS OFF YOU!

The Youth Executive Council has voted to add an extra room for the Sunday evening program. We now have the combined rooms in Gilbert Hall for youth meetings.

DON'T THINK OF THIS AS WAY OVER YOUR HEAD!

Do you know how many times you share your faith each month? If you're like most of us, you can probably improve.

Why not come to the youth meeting Sunday night where we'll be discussing evangelism?

YOU'LL GET A KICK OUT OF THIS!

The BLUE team was declared the winner in last week's competitions.

Be sure to join us next Wednesday for the semi finals.

TIPS:

TO LAY OUT ANY OF THESE PIECES, THE KEY TO SUCCESS IS TO GET THE ILLUSTRATION TO FIT TIGHTLY WITH THE TYPE. ONE HELP IN PLANNING THE LAYOUTS IS TO USE TRACING PAPER FOR A ROUGH DRAFT.

STEP 1 POSITION THE ART SO THAT IT DOMINATES THE LAYOUT. SIZE IT UP OR DOWN ON YOUR COPIER TO GET THE SIZE THAT YOU WANT.

STEP 2 LAY TRACING PAPER OVER YOUR PAGE AND HANDWRITE YOUR TITLE ON THE TRACING PAPER. NEXT, PLOT THE AVAILABLE SPACE FOR TEXT BY OUTLINING THE AVAILABLE AREA WITH A PENCIL ON THE TRACING PAPER.

STEP 3 LOAD THE TRACING PAPER INTO YOUR TYPEWRITER AND TYPE THE TEXT INSIDE YOUR OUTLINE. (IT MAY TAKE 2-3 TRYS TO GET A GOOD FIT.) NEXT, RETYPE FINAL COPY ON WHITE PAPER; CUT AND PASTE TO THE LAYOUT.

HOOPS ARE HERE!

OUTLINE

WHAT A RACQUET

Last week's rummage sale brought in $600 for the Beach Trip! Thanks to all who helped out.

We'll have more details on the trip next week.

WHAT'S YOUR STYLE?

Everyone has an idea of what they like when they see clip art. Certain styles of art may appeal to them for some occasions but not others.

Here are two styles of clip art used for the same publication. The examples show how the type styles and graphics are changed to complement the style of the illustration.

THIS STYLE IS A MORE SERIOUS APPROACH THAT GIVES THE READER A SENSE OF A NEAT, ORDERLY PROGRAM THAT DOESN'T HAVE TOO MANY FRILLS.

VIKING FOOTBALL

CLARKSVILLE CHRISTIAN HIGH SCHOOL

THE EXAMPLE ON THE RIGHT SHOWS WHAT CAN BE DONE TO MODIFY THE STYLE WITH A FEW SIMPLE CHANGES.

THE HEADLINE TYPE HAS BEEN ALTERED, AS WELL AS THE LINE TREATMENT (SEE 1 AND 2 DETAIL SAMPLES IN CIRCLES), TO GIVE THE PIECE A MORE CASUAL LOOK.

VIKING FOOTBALL

CLARKSVILLE

1. ON A LIGHT TABLE (OR WINDOW) TRACE THE TYPE WITH STRAIGHT, ANGULAR STROKES.

2. ONCE YOU'VE OUTLINED THE TYPE AND DARK BACK-GROUND, FILL IT IN SOLID. USE A FINE-POINT FELT-TIP PEN. (YOU MAY WANT TO ENLARGE THE TYPE ON YOUR COPIER BEFORE TRACING.)

HOW TO MAKE THE MOST OF YOUR ART

A coordinated system of promotional items will do a lot for your identity. You may not be able to produce all of these at once, but if the planning is done first, then each piece will complement the others.

Colors can be added by hand or can be printed. It's important to have everyone responsible for sports promotion to cooperate in producing a consistent, quality image.

SPORTS PROGRAM

A TEAM ROSTER AND SCHEDULE CAN FIT IN THE GAME PROGRAM. THIS IS PROBABLY THE MOST USED PUBLICATION.

BUTTON

A BUTTON IS ALWAYS GREAT FOR CREATING EXCITEMENT OR FOR A SOUVENIR OF A SPECIAL EVENT.

CENTRAL HIGH SCHOOL
Basketball Season

Monday 7:30 pm
Seat 58
Row 36

CENTRAL
Basketball

Monday 7
Seat 58
Row 36

SEASON TICKET

TICKETS

SOMETIMES TICKETS CAN BE USED AS PROMOTIONAL ITEMS. SCHEDULES CAN BE PRINTED ON THE BACK OF A SEASON TICKET.

FLYER/POSTER

THIS IS ALWAYS THE WORKHORSE FOR COMMUNICATING COMING EVENTS. YOU SHOULD PRODUCE POSTERS AT KEY TIMES BEFORE AN ACTIVITY.

BOOSTER CARD
CENTRAL HIGH SCHOOL
Basketball Season

Monday 7:30 pm
Seat 58
Row 36

BOOSTER CLUB CARD

...A "MEMBERSHIP CARD" TO PROMOTE PARENT PARTICIPATION IN SPORTS.

13

We want to serve you! Send us your ideas so that we can draw them for future books to assist you in your ministry.

Name_____

Church or Ministry_____

Address_____

City_____

State_____Zip_____

Phone_____

B R A I N S T O R M   F O R M

Here are some ideas I'd like to see in future books:

Basketball:

Football:

Miscellaneous:

Soccer:

Softball/Baseball:

Tennis/Racquetball:

Track and Field:

Volleyball/Walleyball:

Copy and send to: The Church Art Works • 875 High Street NE • Salem, Oregon 97301 • (503) 370-9377 • FAX (503) 362-5231

14

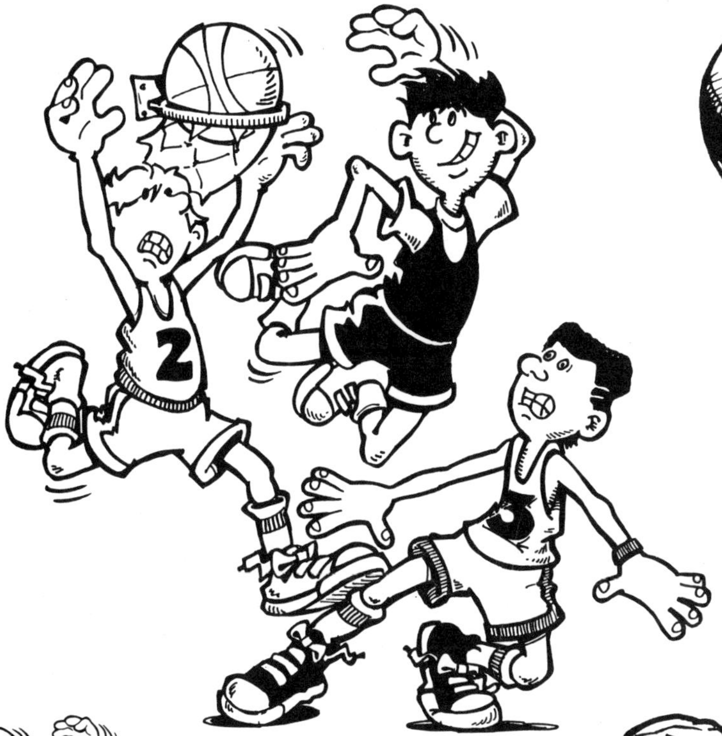
2

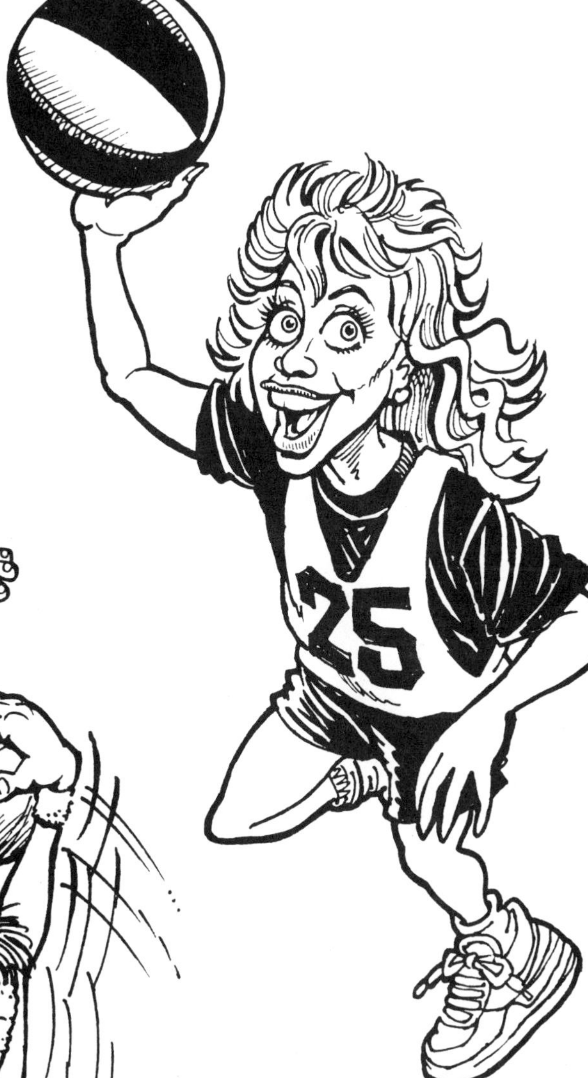
25

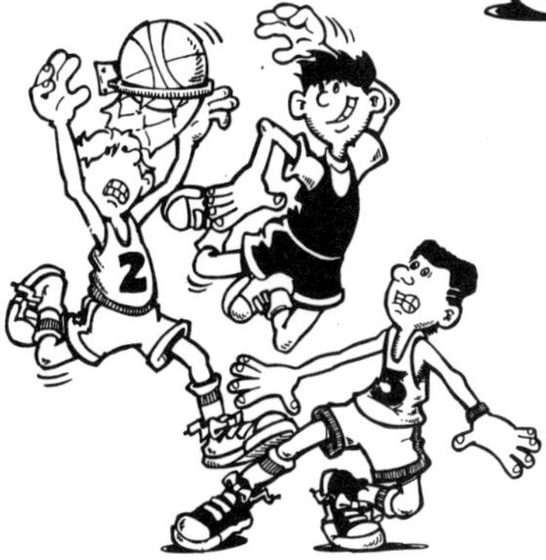
2

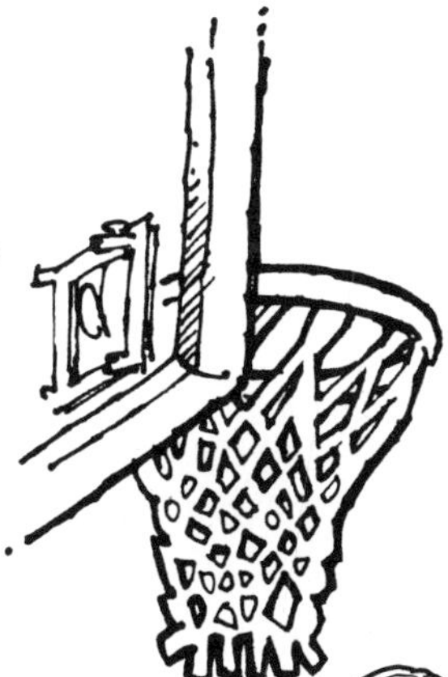

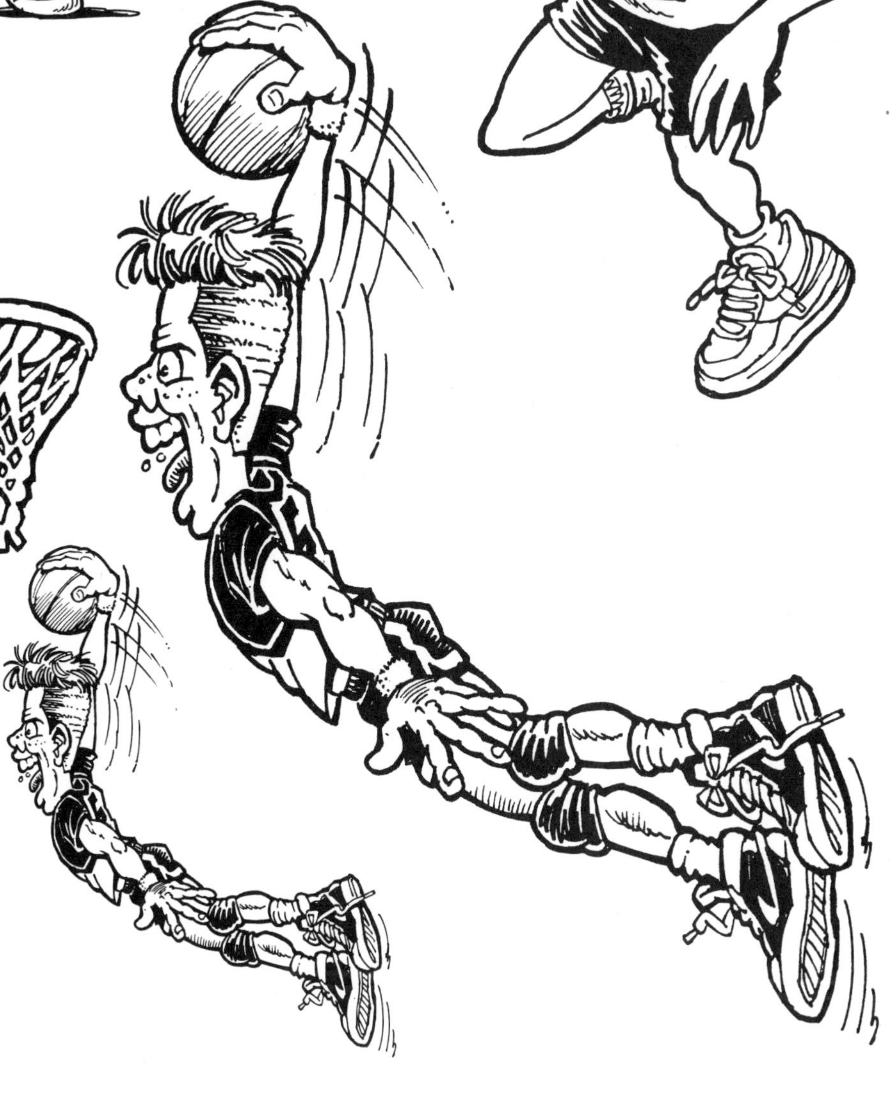

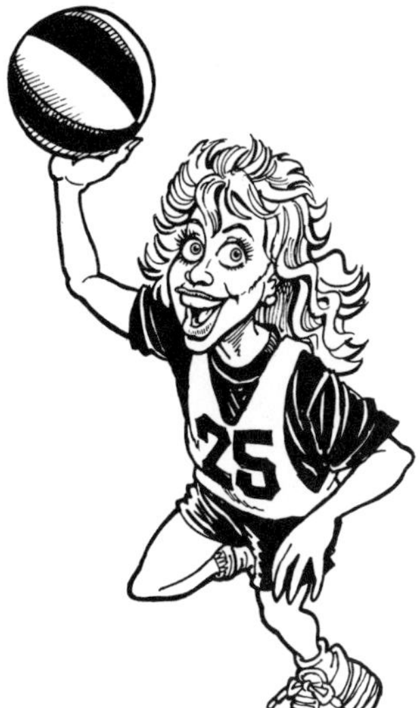
25

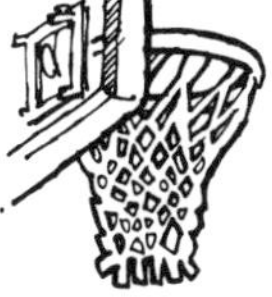

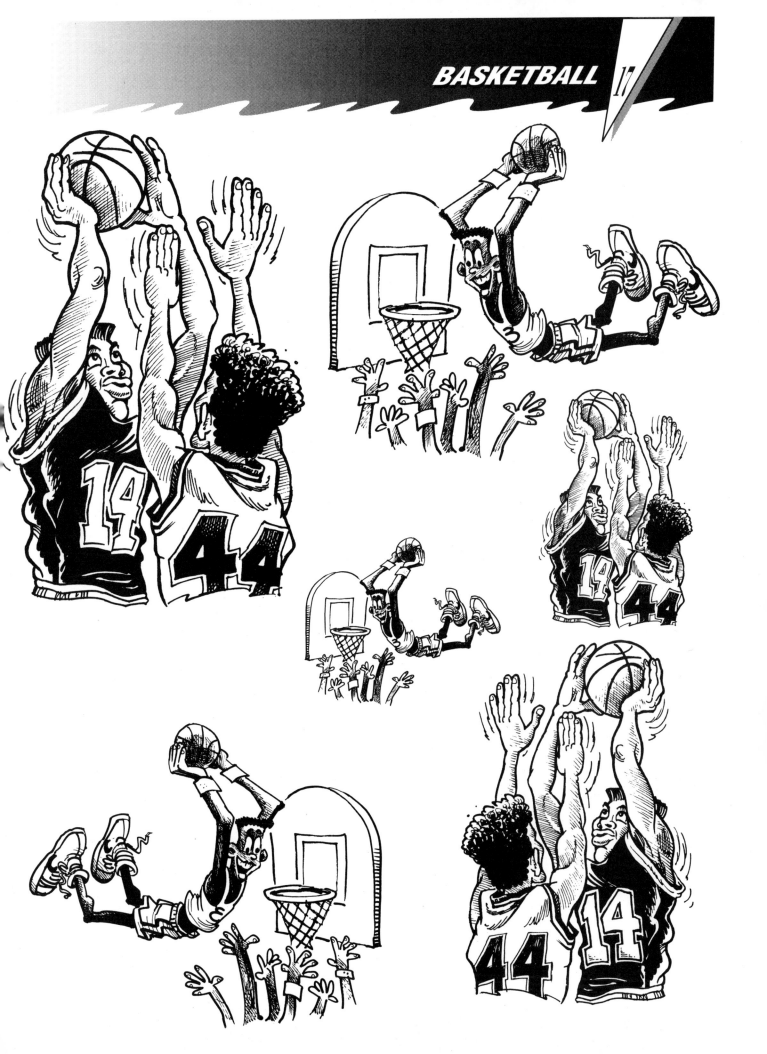

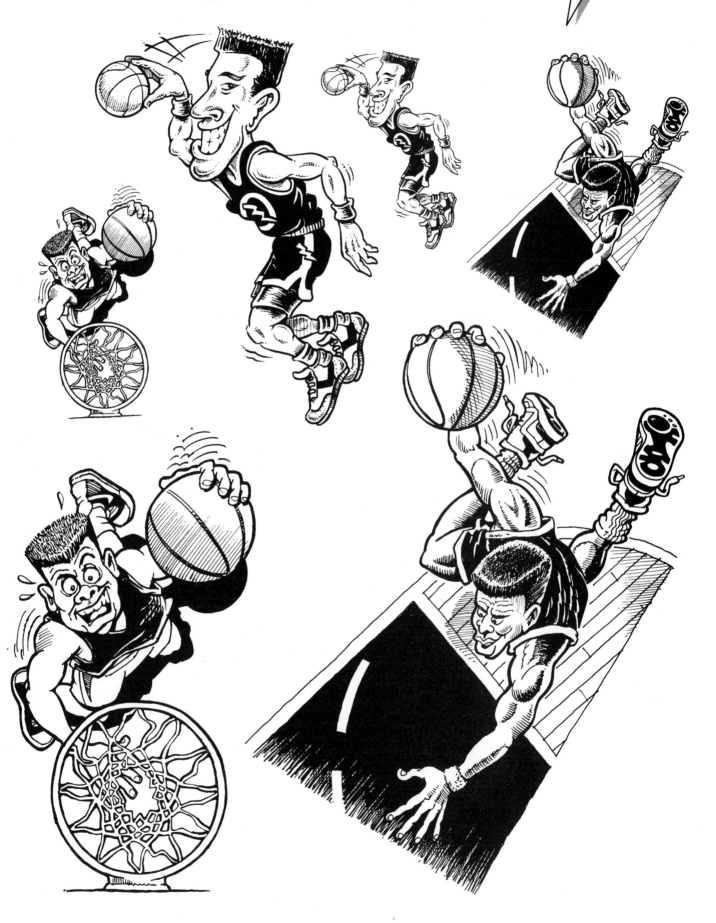

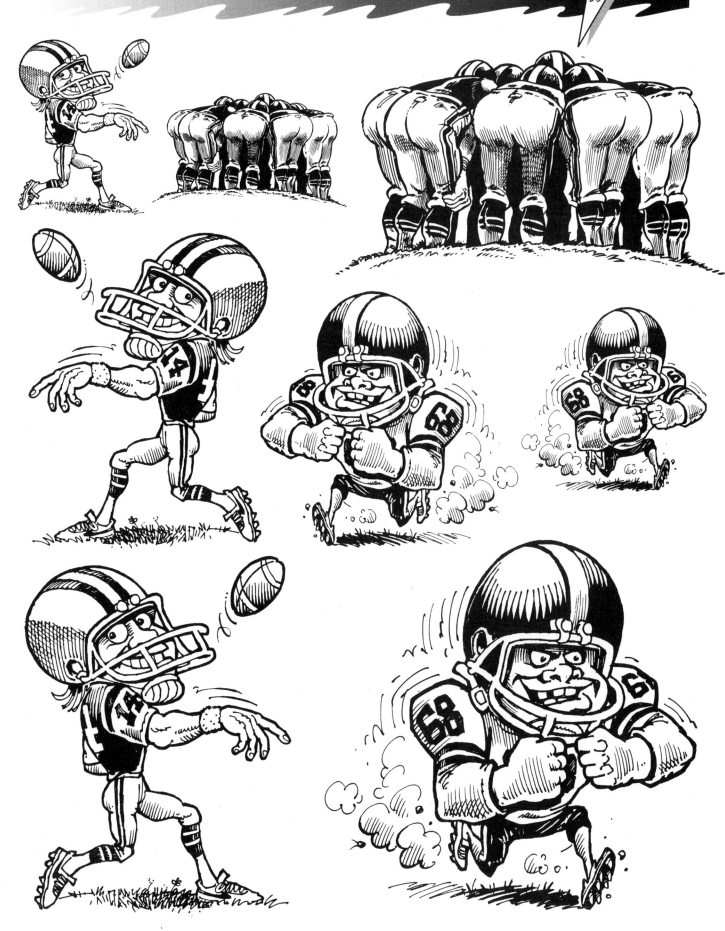

Softball

Softball

SOFTBALL

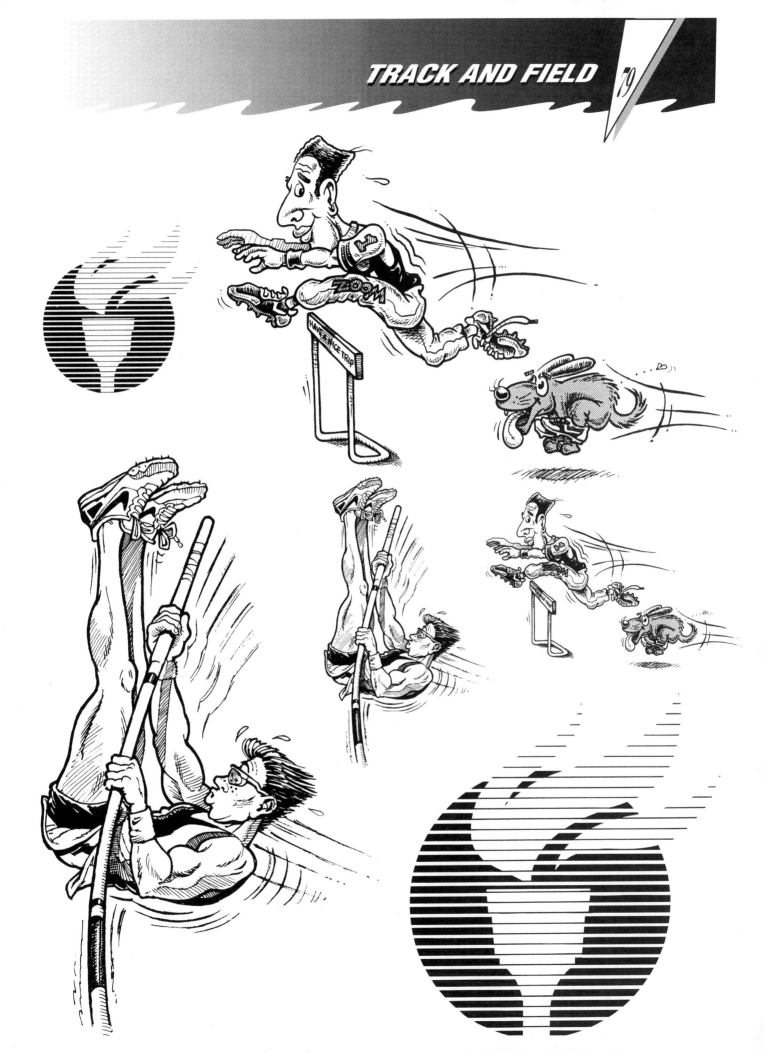

VOLLEYBALL

VOLLEYBALL

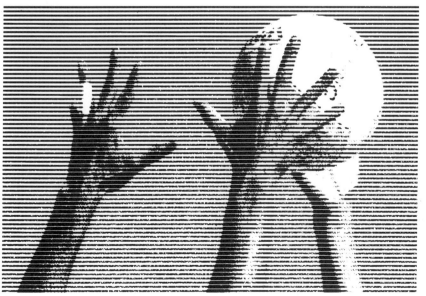